BEYOND THE TRAILHEAD

A POETRY COLLECTION

BEYOND THE TRAILHEAD

A POETRY COLLECTION

CHET DIXON

TWEED PRESS

AN IMPRINT OF
OGHMA CREATIVE MEDIA

Tweed Press
Oghma Creative Media
Fayetteville, Arkansas

www.oghmacreative.com

ISBN: 978-1-63373-122-6

Cover Photo by Greg Smentkowski
Interior Design by Casey W. Cowan
Editing by Diana Ross

ACKNOWLEDGEMENTS
THANKS

I want to thank Diana Ross, my editor, for keeping me from making many errors. I also wish to thank my daughter, Aimee, for making suggestions, asking good questions and typing each poem.

Thanks also to Greg Smentkowski, for his permission to use the breathtaking photo that graces the cover of this work.

If it were possible, I would also thank every individual in person who enriched my life with their presence and nurture. They kept me alive and moving forward, and have impacted my writing immensely. Many individuals have influenced my life and work with their love, companionship and encouragement. This has allowed me to experience this great and wonderful world which offers us freedom to live, grow, and express our feelings, passions, visions, hopes, and dreams. Thank you all!

POEMS

CONTENTS

AUTHOR'S
NOTE

Anyone can come to a trailhead and continue beyond it as far as they wish. However, if they choose to go further, they need to saddle up, or walk. No motor vehicle is allowed. Ahead of you lies the great, vast wilderness. You are free to enter.

The wilderness will greet you with its beauty and independence. You enter on its terms. It offers you adventure and discovery but never protection and sympathy. You are welcomed, but not solicited.

Whether you seek a physical, mental, or spiritual experience you can find it beyond the trailhead. If you savor its magic, mystery, adventure and challenges, it gives healing to the soul and inspiration to the creative, and gives great pleasure to people with a strong outdoor spirit.

If you have never heard the sounds of winds ambling through wilderness high country pine, fir, and quaking aspen groves, you have missed a great experience. These sounds talk and sing to you, create feelings and emotions, while they urge you to tell their story so that others can listen to their voices. No other place will they talk to you as they do in the wilderness woods and high country. As you write and listen, you hear songs with mysterious melodies, and crowds talking. You can hear whispers, as if secrets are being told. You listen and interpret words and tongues never heard. You become a prophet interpreting strange messages. It captures you, and you can experience sadness, happiness, loneliness, and may even weep. You write. The sounds never leave you. You crave more. You keep listening.

I am explaining part of wilderness high country, but only a part. One description can never adequately explain its vastness, remote location, its mystery and majestic beauty. Always remember, the wilderness accepts you willingly but does not cater to your whims or weaknesses. There are dangers, if you are careless. It is filled with surprises that bring alive every human sense. Sometimes it will test your ability to survive.

No matter who you are, young or old, experiences begin just beyond the trailhead that may be old or new, but never without great value. These poems reflect some of the life you will find there. For sure, when you experience life beyond the trailhead, you will anxiously await a return.

Chet Dixon

Go beyond the trailhead
To hunt, fish and hike,
Or go to think
Or sit, read and write.
But for all who go beyond
Will find joy, solitude and rest.
Beyond they'll easily understand
How we all are richly blessed.

FOREWARD
TO THE COLLECTION

The poems in this collection clearly reveal a deep love and understanding of the great outdoors. This love of the wilderness and backcountry of both North and South America no doubt originated in the writer's youth. Chet was born in a log cabin deep in the southern Missouri Ozarks. He went to a one-room school that had 12-18 students each year. While going to grade school, he became the janitor for one whole year, his first real job.

It was in this remote Ozarks setting that he began to write about its romance and adventure. From youth to adulthood, he spent lots of time in the woods along pristine lakes and streams. This instilled a deep desire to capture both their beauty and music for the soul.

In 1950, he wrote his first complete poem. Hundreds of poems later, this collection, *Beyond the Trailhead*, and others are being published.

When Chet was a young boy, there were special places he found inspiring. He would visit them often, in secret. One special place required that he slip out of the house at night and walk through dark woods to his favorite bluff lookout high above the beautiful White River and listen to the rumbling water as it flowed over rocky shoals. Those times at the lookout, he would explain later in his life, inspired him to become a writer.

Even though he had never written anything except what the schoolteacher demanded, he began his first novel at age 12, and then lost his only copy, soon after. It was never recovered, but that experience gave him an open door to imagination and expression never before known to him. It created a great desire to share with others the beauty and tranquility of the Ozarks backcountry.

Poetry is his primary genre of writing other than technical writing relating to his profession and work. Chet has been heard to say that poetry was a valuable asset during his college years. It became a tranquilizer when bad times came around.

He invites you to come along to the backwoods where he has spent lots of time hiking, camping, hunting, and writing. This book, along with others, offers snapshots into the life and thoughts of Chet Dixon, my dad.

Aimee Dixon Plumlee

Dedicated to my loved ones

HIGH COUNTRY
CAMP

Friendly fires glow dimly
As wood in ashes simmers.
The tricky cool creeps
As darkness swallows the world.

Rumbles of the Vallecito grow clearer,
Stars from endless heavens glimmer,
The giant silhouettes huddle in ceremony
As darkness swallows the world.

The secret steps of lowland life move.
Elk herds raid high meadows.
The world both sleeps and awakens
As darkness swallows the world.

Tent life tucks in its bundle
As frost makes an early visit.
All the world is swallowed and touched
Until darkness leaves the world.

BEYOND THE TRAILHEAD
CHET DIXON

 DEEP WOODS

Troubles always send me
Into deep woods,
Mountain woods where
Rivers run still,
Eyes and ears open,
And imprisonment of the soul
Is freed.

In the deep woods
I can hear, see and
Feel safe,
Where chairs are soft
And freedom is abundant
And troubles flee.

SNOWFLAKES
FALLING

Listen closely and you can hear
Snowflakes falling
Their voices so soft
And quietly calling
To other snowflakes
Side by side
Sharing their company
Not wanting to hide.

Listen closely
It's a special sound
Nothing less than
Something profound,
Like a sound of God
In a whispering voice
Saying come to me
And together rejoice.

Just stand in awe
Of a miracle performed
Its greatness and beauty
In an instant born.
No word nor prose
Can describe the sound
That was given so freely
That my soul had found.

BEYOND THE TRAILHEAD
CHET DIXON

ALONE
WITH EVENING

Before my eyes, my fingertips,
And fresh upon my searching lips,
The sound of evening found my stay
And with my guest I went away.

Then my sleep and fevered dreams
Were born upon her soft airstreams.
And in a fleece of sense and sound
My soul came silent my burdens down.

SEASONS

When winter snows come falling down,
Silent and without a sound,
They touch the earth in ancient duty
Together in wondrous finite beauty.

Then soon they quietly disappear
To befriend a beginning new born year
When rains begin just in time
Making a statement of nature's rhyme.

This story so obvious and clear
Gives more to the eye than the ear.
Clearly we can see its earthly form
Yet not understanding its spirit's morn.

We can see the earth get watered and grow,
We joy in its renewal but know,
That the spirit safely hidden away
Will always show its time of day.

Early or late the earth endures.
The war that rages, subtle but sure
Will scar the face that lies beneath us
With no harm done to its godly genius.

NOVEMBER
SURPRISE

It's hard to believe that winter has come
When Spring was here just weeks ago.

Now the cold sends chills right to my bones
As the snow presents its wintry show.

To make this event a little less bruising
I gave thanksgiving to begging squirrels.

Then the weather seemed a little less fearsome
Seeing squirrels eat heartily with tails in swirls.

So now I say on this snow white day
There is much beauty in a November surprise.

It doesn't seem so bad since many don't mind
That Winter came quickly at Fall's quick demise.

BEYOND THE TRAILHEAD
CHET DIXON

HOPE

Fog is floating, the red sun rising,
Morning is cold and still.
Geese are honking, crows are calling,
The osprey displays his stealthy skill.

Unnoticed I'm watching, carefully listening,
As the world takes up its flight.
In all the worlds revealing, the thought is haunting,
That there's coming an endless night.

No matter this thinking, I'll not be waiting,
For some dreadful coming end.
I'll trust in my viewing, that keeps renewing,
The endless hope within.

ALONE

Sometimes you need to be alone
To get back your balance and trim.
You need to get your bones rejoined
And your body sleek and slim.

Sometimes you get overwhelmed
And want to run away.
And when your nights are troubled
The deep woods draw your stay.

Then when its' quietness surrounds you
And its natural treatment is felt,
Your soul begins to rest,
Your unwanted troubles dealt . . .
Disappear.

THE
CROW

I listened to an early noisy crow
That seemed so occupied.
He was telling other crows to come
Or maybe just to hide.

Whatever the truth
His friends came very quick.
Had he sounded an alarm
Or was he just a country hit?

It didn't take long
For their chatter to cease.
But my ears and eyes kept searching
For another top release.

Then at last I heard them,
They erupted to restore
The hype of one crow
And now, his noisy encore.

BEYOND THE TRAILHEAD
CHET DIXON

WILD PLACES

Wild places
Where rushing waters
Run deep,
And mountains rise steep,
Where secret trails
Take walkers,
Both beast and prey,
To places hunted
Both night and day.

The breath of wild places,
Sounds of its sleep,
Reveal deep shadows
Of invading things,
With strange names
And violent wishes,
To change its lore
Its mystery,
Its miracles.

It tells us
We have debts to pay
Starting today.
Shadows creeping
Will not stop.
If my eyes
Fail to see
This timid me
Will need to be food
For waiting vultures,
As wild places ....disappear.

BEYOND THE TRAILHEAD
CHET DIXON

PERFECT
L O V E

When rains kiss the ground
And winds embrace the trees
That's when we understand
That God has breathed.

HIGH COUNTRY

Untamed as skies
The mountains rise
To cloudy mystery,
And hunters surmise
It is easily tamed.

When one day ends
With sore, tired feet
The hunters descend,
Where valleys greet
With unbelieved pleasure.

A look back up
Where the mountains rise,
A truth is found.
The hunters know
They are still untamed.

DREAMING
OF ELK COUNTRY

Every December I get an urge
To backtrack the October hunt.
It must be the spirit of Christmas
And people asking what I want
That kindles a craving
For one more hunt.

When I read the latest BUGLE
And watch the snows swirl round,
I sense the smell of pine and fir
And hear the aspen leaves falling down,
Making a forest carpet
At the foot of teasing peaks

In my sleep at night I keep dreaming
Of rival bulls mocking,
And hearing those strange sounds
Of the high country winds talking
And sharing with me
Mysteries of elk country.

This December I will only sit and read
And periodically call my prey
As I sit here on my back porch
Anticipating a coming day,
When back up the trail I'll go
To secret places that only
My prey and I know.

BEYOND THE TRAILHEAD
CHET DIXON

A WINTER
S P E L L

Storm clouds came with sheets of snow
Coming in late one wintry night.
So soft and silent it floated down
Making ghostly cover all around.

When morning came the cedars hovered
And flocks of robins noisily fed.
In perfect harmony the world stood quiet
As the heavens and earth ceremoniously wed.

This happy magic of beauty and cold
Reflected the aura of new found lovers.
The cedars, the robins gathered as mates
In commune with majestic winter covers.

The morning cleared to cloudless skies
Basking in silent rich delight.
My spirit then lifted far beyond
The world of beauty wrapped in white.

WINTER
WOODS

The snow is falling
Covering the pines and cedars white.
The woods are lit by the moon's eerie flight
And shadows wait.

The cold wail of wolves
Echoes through the meadows now still,
As hunters listen, dreaming to fill
Their driven mission.

The winter covers the world
And slumber fills the camp with dreams,
Of strategies and hunting schemes
For tomorrow.

But this night belongs to wolves.
They own the meadows, valleys, and hills
And I will listen, or sleep, but be still
Until I claim my ground.

SACRED
RACE

The prey was near
In open breeze
I dared not cough
I dared not sneeze.

I heard his steps
In the hidden lair
Away from danger
Of an arrows flair.

The gentle breeze
To my favor sped
And brought my prey
Where wild things fed.

Just like a prince
He came so brave
Testing my resolve
His life to save.

With my sole intent
To fulfill a duty
He stirred my soul
With his natural beauty

My arrow ready
To speed away
Did not go flying
But let him stay

BEYOND THE TRAILHEAD
CHET DIXON

Like a brother,
He touched my soul
And doused the hunters
Natural goal.

The gentle breeze
Once in my favor
Turned toward him
With rich human flavor

Danger he sensed
Was very near
He bounded away
With deathly fear

Then I sat
To consider the event
The dilemma I faced
A confusion to vent

What is happening
To my way of life
To seek my prey
Then pocket my knife

I'd watched him often
To get the chance
To successfully do
My spiritual dance

Then with a smile
And a breeze in my face
I walked away knowing
We both won a race.

BEYOND THE TRAILHEAD
CHET DIXON

STREAM

Trickling stream
As cotton spun,
It and I
Merged as one,
Makes me feel
Twix and tween
Love real
And love a dream.

Trickle over stones
And through the trees
Go with your strength
Forever free.
Trickling stream
Never stop flowing
Give us your medicine
But go where you're going.

Oh, trickling stream
As cotton spun,
You and I have
Merged as one.
You always make me feel
Locked in between
Love real
And love in my dreams.

ALONG
A ROAD

When I stopped along a road today
To sit and rest while,
Instead of hurrying on,

I knew that on ahead were other gems
To catch my mind and soul
But not like here alone.

Beside a weeping willow grove
Framing a rippling pool and mill,
I felt a sense of bliss.

I looked closely, listened well,
Knowing the little time I spend
Would be a time I'd never miss.

Now I look closely every time
At every stopping place
To find its value to share.

And when my life has lost control
I stop along some road and sit
Until it takes the weight I bear.

BEYOND THE TRAILHEAD
CHET DIXON

SONG

When fires rage around me
And lions walk on both sides
When captured and bound in chains
And there's no place to run or hide
I know He lives within me
And walks here by my side
I will have no shame or fear
I have no reason to hide.

No matter how big my troubles
Or how bound I am in chains
My God is always with me
He gives me everything
He quietly stands beside me
His peace He freely gives
No danger or threat can touch me
Because He really lives.

I know He lives within me
And He walks by my side
I have no shame or fear
I have no reason to hide

I have no shame or fear
I have no reason to hide.

FACES
OF NIGHT

Listen to night voices,

Open your silent ear.

Listen to them saying

Come be near.

I have much to tell you.

A DANCE
ON ICE

My dreams
Went dancing
On a blanket of ice.

They sped
Across a valley
On a silver glare.

I sailed
Without fear
In perfect stride,

And never
Wished to stop
My magical dare.

For in
That moment
All clocks had stopped,

As I sailed alone
In icy space
Until the world adjourned.

The miracle
Quietly ended
The real came back,

And the piece of heaven
Departed,
And never returned.

Yet another dance
Lies waiting
Ahead in my path.

It's just beyond
My human view
But advancing.

Soon my dream
Will again
Reappear,

And together
We will glide
Across heaven—
Dancing.

HIGH COUNTRY
MOMENT

We climbed mountains
Where skies are held
By snow peak stilts.

We climbed mountains
Where pathways find light
From trusted stars.

We climbed mountains
And waited, and sang
And watched the earth breathe.

Now up high I close my eyes
And keep climbing
To where I find you.

MIRACLE

Beside a crackling glowing fireside
With dim glows drifting across the woods,
Voice muffled low.

Stars flickered between leafy limbs,
The cool breezes meandered
As if not knowing where to go.

Night hawks gave their eerie sounds
Free and without knowing
Where their voices would end.

Then with the passing universe
Voices became quiet and watchful
Seeking not to offend,
A miracle passing by.

THE SOURCE

Be still,
Go beyond where noises capture
And consume your space.

Go where senses bow
To the mastery of silence,
Where understanding grows
And focus is crowned.

Honor your natural gifts
And be taught by their truth,
Never altered by change.

Feed the soul from the source
Untangled by the smog
That disguises and destroys
What is real.

SOUL FOOD

Hungry for the silent hills
And feeling senses not pristine
I walked the sketchy hillside round
And found nothing yet unseen.

But as the dusk began to fall
And chilly winds began their search,
I heard a melody
Of the evening, suddenly perch,

Upon my hungering—
Then I was fed.

SECOND SONG

Oh Lord I cry out
And search for You
Lift me up
And make me new.

My heart is heavy
I've a burdened soul
Come dear Lord
Come make me whole.

(chorus)
You made me from dust
And breathed life into me
So that I could have life
And have it free
You gave me all
That I could ever need
Oh Lord I come now
My soul to feed.

There's no other source
Of freedom and love
It's so abundant and pure
And it comes from above.

You care for my soul
You wait for my plea
So Lord, my dear Lord,
I surrender to Thee.

(chorus)
You made me from dust
And breathed life into me
So that I could have life
And have it free
You gave me all
That I could ever need
Oh Lord I come now
My soul to feed.

Praise and thanks I humbly give
I praise You now because You live
You gave me all I'll ever need
Oh Lord, I come, my soul to feed

Yes, Lord, You are my every source
You watch and wait for me
So right now my Lord
I surrender all to Thee.

(chorus)
You made me from dust
And breathed life into me
So that I could have life
And have it free
You gave me all
That I could ever need
Oh Lord I come now
My soul to feed.

BEYOND THE TRAILHEAD
CHET DIXON

TRANSFORMATION

Along a leaning wetted glade
I found a path that deer had made.
The hovering cedars reaching far
And matted grasses the view to mar,
Shielded from all intruders.

They lay there quietly safe in hiding
Looking upon a valley and a hill.
And even though they had it marked
They endlessly watched, ever still,
Knowing there are intruders.

But hearing my footsteps along the glade
They scurried from their shelter made.
And found I only a trace of life
And not the fresh blood from my knife,
That pierces springing veins.

Then I crawled beneath the cedar
Hovering the earth about one meter.
I sat upon the fresh deer beds
To feel the meadow and heat they shed,
Before I had alarmed them.

And there along the wetted glade
Upon the mats my prey had made.
I found a self remotely hiding
Carefully wrapped in safe abiding,
And kept from all intruders.

MEADOWLARK

Today I walked to an open field
To listen to the songs of the meadowlark.
His songs brought peace and quiet
Where life had become lost and dark.

His songs rang out so melodious and clear
And made me understand that I was free.
I stood listening to his transforming songs
And realized this medicine was meant for me.

OCTOBER

Falling to silence
But not obeying
They lie;
Ready to rush
With childish gaiety,
Mischievously,
But not away.

Even in this sadness
Merges she to nature
In charity;
But for awhile,
Wildly running,
Playing,
Crackling with joyous
Autumnal tones,
She speeds away…
Sheepishly.

Oh Mother
Of Autumn charm
Be not saddened
As they run away.
Desertion has
Its needed season.
Tomorrow

BEYOND THE TRAILHEAD
CHET DIXON

A new sun
Will awaken you,
And again,
Rising splendor
Will caress your
Sleeping lids
For another walk,
And another season.

FLY

O N

Robins in flight
To fields they go
Where they will land
I really don't know

Driven by a spirit
Of a heavenly choir
I wait here watching
Safe by the fire

They surely are driven
By what I can't see
But whatever it is
It's filled with glee

I see it in their eyes
When they land in my tree
Oh my friends, go quickly
Fly on from me

The fields are ripe and waiting
To fill your great desire
But fly back my good friend
I'll be waiting by the fire

Fly on to your dream

BEYOND THE TRAILHEAD
CHET DIXON

To your own promised land
Through clear skies and storms
Never ceasing to stand

Go on, fly to your fields
With all your chirps and chime
Others there are feasting
Do not waste your time!

I'll keep watching your flight
As far as I can see
Fly on my good friend
You can know where I'll be

I'll just wait…..

Here by the fire.

For Nate, on his 5th Birthday.

Chet
1-1-11

THOUGHTS

Meditating, I embraced a thought,
For no one had talked
To scurry it away without me.

Then I met a man,
With an outstretched hand,
At the streetside, wishing.

He said, "My gentle friend,
Upon men like you, I depend."
"Would you give to my misfortune?"

The time parcel asked of me
Was so little for charity
Yet, more than it I pursued.

"Thank you, my good Sir," he said,
"With this I'll soon be fed.
May your walk bring good cheer."

Looking about for my thoughts
That solitude once had brought,
I silently became fearful and lonely.

It had bid me good day,
Not tolerant of my stay,
For I had become unreverent.

The vagabond, mumbling as to say,
This is surely my day,
Found joy in his thoughts.

His steps pressed into the snow
Told the path he would go,
But my thoughts had no prints.

Vagabond, thought, and charity gone,
I then walked alone...   Wishing...

CHANGE

My courtship with time
Makes me chase wild turkey at night
My flight becomes bold and fervent
Like a young soldier
My muscles become firm
Like a logger's arm, and
With ease I swing the twelve-gauge
Like a broken Johnson weed.

My courtship with time
Makes me chase wild turkey at night
As I grow in age and wisdom
And feast upon an odious diet
Of time and change not requested
But growing.

My courtship with time
Keeps me hunting at night
And wondering.
Will daylight return
So that I can
hunt again?

THE
CHASE

We ran the monarch through the fields
And into deep dark woods.
We ran in vain to copy his flight
To catch him if we could.

My friend ran on as I turned away
To allow him to go alone.
I waited quietly and searched the sky
For other monarchs going home.

Not yielding to the folly of one or nothing
The monarchs came in crowds of gold,
And on my outstretched hand they lit
And there a story told.

To run with blinders fills no need
For there are many roads to joy
You need to look at the monarch's flight
To discover God's great toy

My heart felt joy as I silently watched
A marvelous parade crossing the sky.
And my tranquil silence was briefly disturbed
As my friend came running by.

COUNTRY
SPRING

Beside a sleepy silent spring
Beneath the hovering oak and pines
A million years of time passed
As memory cradled bygone times.

Here alone in nature's womb
Depending upon its mother's arms,
An image like a newborn child
Found freedom and hillside charm.

Yet loath it does the solid earth
Till time gives out its gentle kiss,
And wraps its arms in cradling love
Beneath its molding gentle hiss.

TRAVELERS

A monarch, coasting, took
The Campbell south alone, and
Had a place well in mind to land.

But in the middle
Of his path obscure, his
Sudden death was hard to understand.

Another traveler,
Destined to his goal, met
The monarch on that day.

Instead of gentle, quiet hellos,
They met head on, not
Giving the right of way.

Maybe not so hidden is a simple story
Of life and death meeting,
And how they never miss a stride.

It shows how the stream
We choose is often filled
With goings against the tide.

HOUNDS
RUNNING

The hounds are running
The chase is on
The chorus is rising.

The hunters are listening,
Ears straining,
To each there's no surprising.

The chase is on
Echoes rising
Making an orchestra in flight.

The hounds are running,
Hunters delighting
In songs of the wistful night.

On they run
As stars kept passing
Growing eager to win the race.

On to morning
With sun rising
Racers knew their coming fate.

BEYOND THE TRAILHEAD
CHET DIXON

44

Running hounds are tiring
Feet growing sore
But instincts deeply bedded,

In blood and bone,
A running spirit
Forever with nature, wedded.

HIGH

TIDE

Along the Beaver Woods I glided
On tops of trees and places high
Where once I walked not far below
But now like birds I fly

My wings now touch where giants hid
To feed upon a likely prey
But below where my world now hides
Is where I would run and play

My wings stroke on like birds of prey
Like soaring eagles flying low
And on I went through sycamore tops
And nature's miraculous show

DUKE

When it's time to say goodbye to
A very special friend who
In your heart has a special place,
You just need to take a walk on
Familiar trails and remember
Them as trails of grace.

You try to disguise feelings
And believe it doesn't matter,
For it's no different than before.
But when eyes look deep inside
The soul and you feel nearness, and
Sadness of what's in store,

You share an embrace.
You say,
Goodbye, my dear friend.

ROBINS

In cedar tops
Robins fed
With all their hype and grace

Unnoticed I
In silence watched
With a smile upon my face

Beholding its beauty
A million times
Transfixed without a move

Time had stopped
For a simple treasure
This moment I would not lose

Then in unison
They filled the skies
And on they went away

But for a while
They came to me
To share a joyous winter day

SNOWFLAKES

Snowflakes in May
Came coasting down
Their spirits hovering
On leaves and ground.
They greeted all guests
Who were passing by
Offering no regrets
Or answers why.

They just kept falling
Their order ordained
As a piece of heaven
On Earth now born.
But it's May time now
The winter is done.
Snow has already gone-----
Except,
This one.

DEER

Deer came feeding by my door
Bringing memories long before
In my hiding they came so near
Without their pristine guarded fear
And lest I scare them I waited long
Until I knew they had quietly gone
And again I wait another day
Patiently hoping they'll come my way

THE
OLD TREE

It's ragged, barren stoic shape
Is going its sleepy way
With fruit now hiding in the grass
To live until another day.

The time has come to say goodbye
To the colors and charms we know
A happy time to feel and see
As it slowly, slowly goes.

Then when no dress is left to see
It will meditate on winter's guest.
And await in silence with lifted arms
And whispering to its guests,

Come rest on my arms once more
And view your world below.
You can safely do your own thing here
And freely come and go.

The whole world knows I'll come awake
To play my role once more
I'll flower and give a birth of life
For all the earth to adore.

BEYOND THE TRAILHEAD
CHET DIXON

CAT
AND TURTLE

One morning I observed an unlikely pair
Sipping milk and nibbling on a slice of bread.
A turtle on the left, a cat on the right
Eye to eye, head to head, with total attention
Ate and drank all they were fed.

The slow stoic strokes of the turtle's head,
The cat's stare and sips,
Made me wonder why this meeting
And whether somewhere along life's trip
They had met and now had notes to compare.

Maybe they were brothers conversing
Tolerant that each has an equal right
To live in peace though different
Not inciting a bloody fight.

STORMS
OF APRIL

Storm nights in April
With thunder and streaks
Across the sky,
Make me contemplate
How God is in control
And how I need not ask-
How or why.

THE EAGLE
AND THE FISH

The eagle had its prey in view
And with stealth
Made his move.

Then the challenge began its course
One would win
The other lose.

What a plan of flesh and blood
One will give
The other take.

Oh how odd this circumstance
That God has chosen
To make.

The one a majestic beauty in flight
The other
A swimmer of grace.

Why do they both exist to give
A lingering dilemma
For my watchful face?

The turmoil raged deep within
Untouchable and
Failed to cease.

I even cover my eyes and plug my ears
But it only
Seems to increase.

Then I heard a small voice say,
It's OK
This natural act.

There is no reason for grieving here
It's only nature's
Surviving act.

Back on the road to normal chores
A cool breeze
Began to lift

The spirit that felt the pain I saw
Was only of nature's
Natural gift.

TIME

I can't believe this tree
Is getting tall and old.
Just a little time ago
I could reach its very top.

But there is a simple lesson
That I've learned very well.
This growing up and old
Will never, never stop,

For both of us.

CROWS

When I gave a piece of bread
To my black feathered friend
He took so little time
To call in all his kin

So quickly they came calling
To share what I shared
Then he and I were pleased
To know we both had cared

RETREAT

Gentle breezes shift the sand
Into mounds of change
That never still,

As the footprints of our lives
Forever shift from
Early morning Sun,

To the first hours of darkness
When they will shift
No more,
Forever.

ICE

Ice clinging
to hanging limbs
Came so quietly
in the dead of night.

It gripped the earth
and time seemed to stop
But knew
Its useless fight.

Soon its shining face
quickly fell away
To continue
Its endless race,

To still new vistas
That beckon on
To a destined place
Of nature's face.

The pain it left
was surely real
Then went by
when the sun appeared.

With laughter and words
the story was told
As the beast of beauty
And the day we had feared.

BEYOND THE TRAILHEAD
CHET DIXON

59

THE SONG
OF THE HOUNDS

The songs of hounds
In distant fields
Bring memories of
A younger chase,

When moonlight spread
Across the hills
And night spirits grew
In a pristine hallowed place.

With eager anticipation
Men often took hounds
Into familiar places
Where resided their friend and foe.

Soon a trail of a beast
Was marked with a howl.
The chase was on and
The beast would scowl!

Across the fields and
Down in the valleys deep
The chase seemed endless
Deeper in the darkest steep.

BEYOND THE TRAILHEAD
CHET DIXON

The listeners waited and warmed
With backs to a fire
And staring at the stars
As it quietly inspires.

They knew each howl and
What it meant.
To the master it was
A clear message sent,

Saying I'm on his tail.
He'll not get away.
Don't tire of my howling
I'll go until I bay.

Listeners keep listening closely.
Oh yeah! That's my hound.
He's out in front and leading.
The trail is fresher and sound.

They listen and keep
Hoping their dog's out ahead.
But no one's ever sure what's
Happening, just hoping instead.

Soon nothing is heard.
Eyes and ears pierce the dark.
That beast has surely taken
Them far away to another part.

BEYOND THE TRAILHEAD
CHET DIXON

They may turn back
Or just keep the chase.
The listeners grow quiet,
Retracing and capping the race.

Sometime before light the
Listeners ready for home.
They douse out the fire
And look again at the starry dome.

The hounds may return
To go home with their master
Or just keep on running
A little slower, never faster.

The stories of the hunt may
Go on for a week,
With each master bragging
About his dog, never meek.

Even now, decades have
Come and gone,
But the memory of hound songs
Are etched in stone.

Even when at night a chase
Rings across my hill,
I listen ever so closely
To what lingers still.

It's the sound of music
And the joy of the chase.
It's the song of hounds
That fills my space.

RAINDROP

One little drop
On a leaf of green
Hardly makes a difference
Or that's the way it seems.

Two little drops
Begin to make a puddle.
I begin to see a difference
But it must not befuddle.

Then it began to shower
Too many drops to count.
And as I watched in silence
My thoughts began to mount.

I'm just a drop of rain
Upon a dusty Earth.
Alone I'm not too great
Unless I know my worth.

Many drops of rain
Along with my little one,
Can make the Earth grow green
Or make a river run.

But when I save my raindrop
To let it live alone,
How much can one raindrop do
When others all have gone?

The destiny of each little life
That God created to be,
Can live and die alone
Or join the power of we.

Desperate is the time we spend
Just being one so quiet,
When the world around us descends
Deep into night.

The life and light of one raindrop
Can make the world grow green.
And when it joins the challenge
It grows what lives in dreams.

One little raindrop we know
Has its sacred place,
Where it can make a difference
On Earth, in time, and space.

IN THE FORK ROAD

We often come to forks in our road
And we have to choose
Which one will make us win
And which will make us lose.

We've all been there one time in life
And were forced to make a choice.
We sometime sought help from others
Or listened to the inner voice.

The inner voice spoke without sound,
"Come, this way is right.
The other way may sound better
But it leads to the darkest night."

The one we choose may be unclear
Requiring us to carefully think
How best to travel its unknown path
Not daring a single blink.

Then as our steps become more sure
We realize a miracle was born.
The road we chose to take was right
Even if not well worn.

So when roads appear and make us choose
Which road is for sure the best.
Just stop and listen to the voice
That will help us pass the choosing test.

I know there's one thing for sure
As I make each difficult choice.
I may listen to good advice
But primarily listen to that inner voice.

THE
S T R E A M

The wind moved
Lightly through the trees
And the sun sat red
In the west.

The moon rose slowly
Above darkened hills
And along this tranquil stream
I loathed the coming test,

Yet I waited.

Beyond my open view
Distant flashes appeared.
In the quiet night
I could only wait and hope.

Soon the trickling sound
Will surely grow and change
And the rush of turbid water
Will test my skills to cope,

Yet I waited.

Night songs in the cooling evening
Quickly brought slumber and rest
And chased the thoughts
Of fear and harm away.

Not until a growing sound
Of water moving fast
Did the unseen spirit
Wake my sleeping stay

To alert me.
Rushing water came near
Filled with mud and trees.
They came along my path
As if to say, move out!

Swiftly and carefully
I moved to higher ground
While harm so near
Again gave a pristine shout,

Move out!

As darkened water kept coming,
Passing without a care,
I quickly folded my tent and bed
And grabbed my boat afloat.

To higher ground I fled
To where I thought it safe,
As rushing turbid water
Seemed to gloat,

BEYOND THE TRAILHEAD
CHET DIXON

At my misfortune.

Not too soon the morning rose
To give a welcome but show no shame.
Everything but water seemed
Happy for the new day.

But all around me
Water harsh and unconcerned
Went by uncaring
On its destined way,

Not mine.

THE
R I V E R

The flood came with reckless fury
Coming at night when people slept.
Its rage struck fear and pain
Across the land and they cursed it.

All earth stood watchfully still and
Helpless until the words of a child moved them.
"Mommy, why did we build farms and houses here?"
"Didn't we know the river had nowhere to go?"

The river raged on until one day
Its tranquility came again
And people played in it, fishermen fished,
Farmers plowed, planted
And reaped a good harvest.

The river became friendly with
Playing, fishing and farming.
Everything was peaceful
And all lived in harmony,

One day the river needed its path
That others had borrowed.
The river covered the land
But trespassed not up on its neighbors.

OF  SPRINGTIME

Her strings are like a violin
Each having its special tune.

And just as music from a master,
The melody stops too soon.

CHET
DIXON

het Dixon grew up in the Ozarks backcountry. He was born in a log cabin built by his father and went to a one room school house that had 12-18 students each year. He considers growing up in the country a rich background for his life of work and writing.

Among a wide range of jobs, he worked with migrant workers in the fruit harvests of Oregon and Washington and as a fishing guide on Missouri lakes and rivers. He has worked for city and state governments in leadership positions. He was also a consultant to the Missouri Women's Council of the Missouri Department of Economic Development. He is a businessman and President of Ministries of Love, Inc., an organization that builds Christian schools in Chile, South America.

His publications include *Learning, Changing, Leading: Keys to Success in the 21st Century* co-authored by Chet Dixon and Sue McDaniel. They also co-authored fifteen other training documents used for consulting work with the Missouri Women's Council.

The author has the strong belief that we all must never stop learning, changing, and leading as the increasingly complex 21st century looms big in our future.

www.chetdixonpoet.com
www.blog.chetdixonpoet.com

Made in the USA
Middletown, DE
12 April 2021